PRODUCER:
CAROLYN FISHER

Let's move it, people!

Sous-chef:
SNOW WHITE

Sous-chef:
JACK FROST

Harcourt, Inc.   Orlando   Austin   New York   San Diego   London   Manufactured in China

Here are today's
INGREDIENTS:
(available in your better latitudes)

WIND

DIRECTIONS

First,
WARM
SOME
WATER

with SUNSHINE.

I love being a big star!

Watch as the water turns from liquid

FLY *the* water vapor

VAPOR - HEAT = WATER
This is called **CONDENSATION**

WATER - HEAT = ICE
This is called **FREEZING**

high in the sky.

Did I mention that I'm afraid of heights?

Reserve some vapor for later use.
Then chill the rest
until it turns into
floating drops of water or ice.

The bunches of floating drops are called...

Bump a water vapor molecule

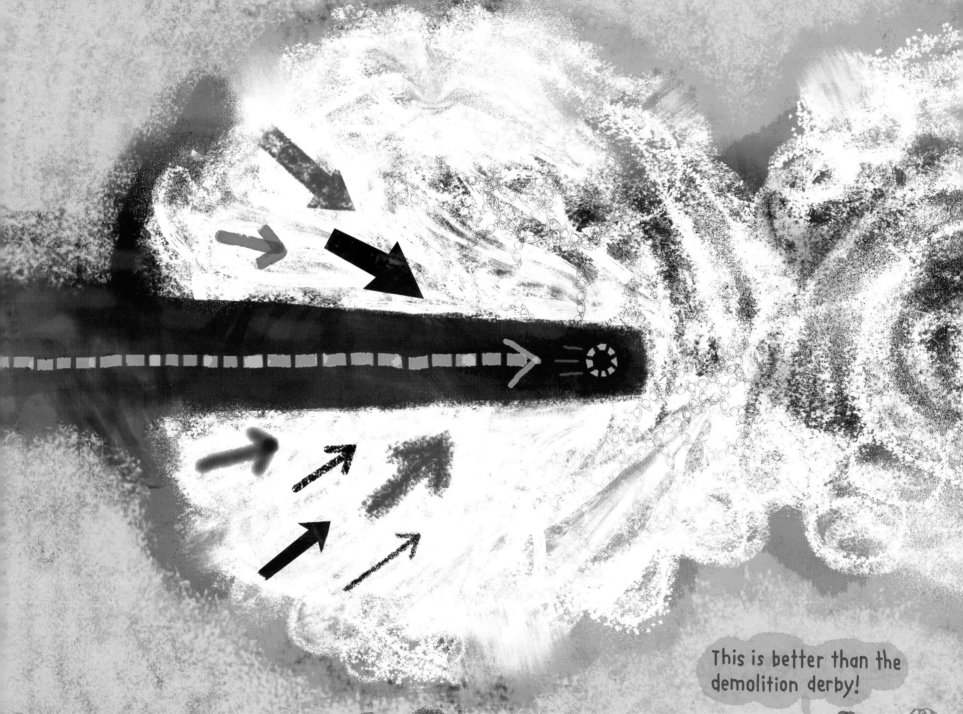

nto a speck of ice or dust.

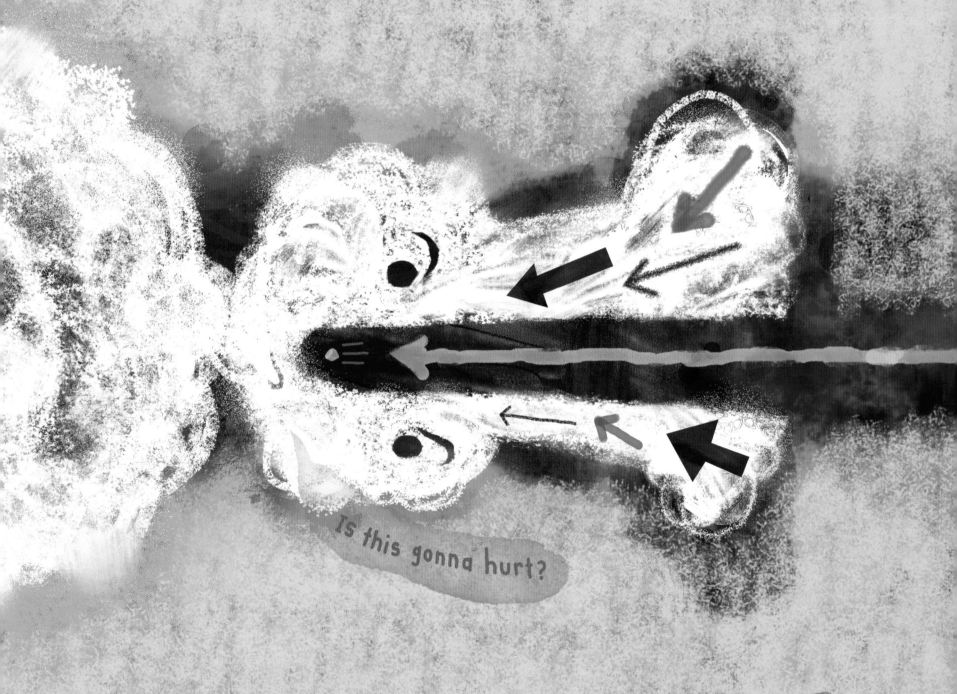

When **VAPOR** TURNS TO **ICE** without turning to liquid,

that's called deposition.

Ice made by deposition grows into...

Snow crystals have a special six-sided shape.

That's because of the way water vapor molecules stack when they freeze.

Snow crystals often look the same from every side.

That's a dirty lie! I'm far handsomer than the other sides!

Now, feed more water vapor

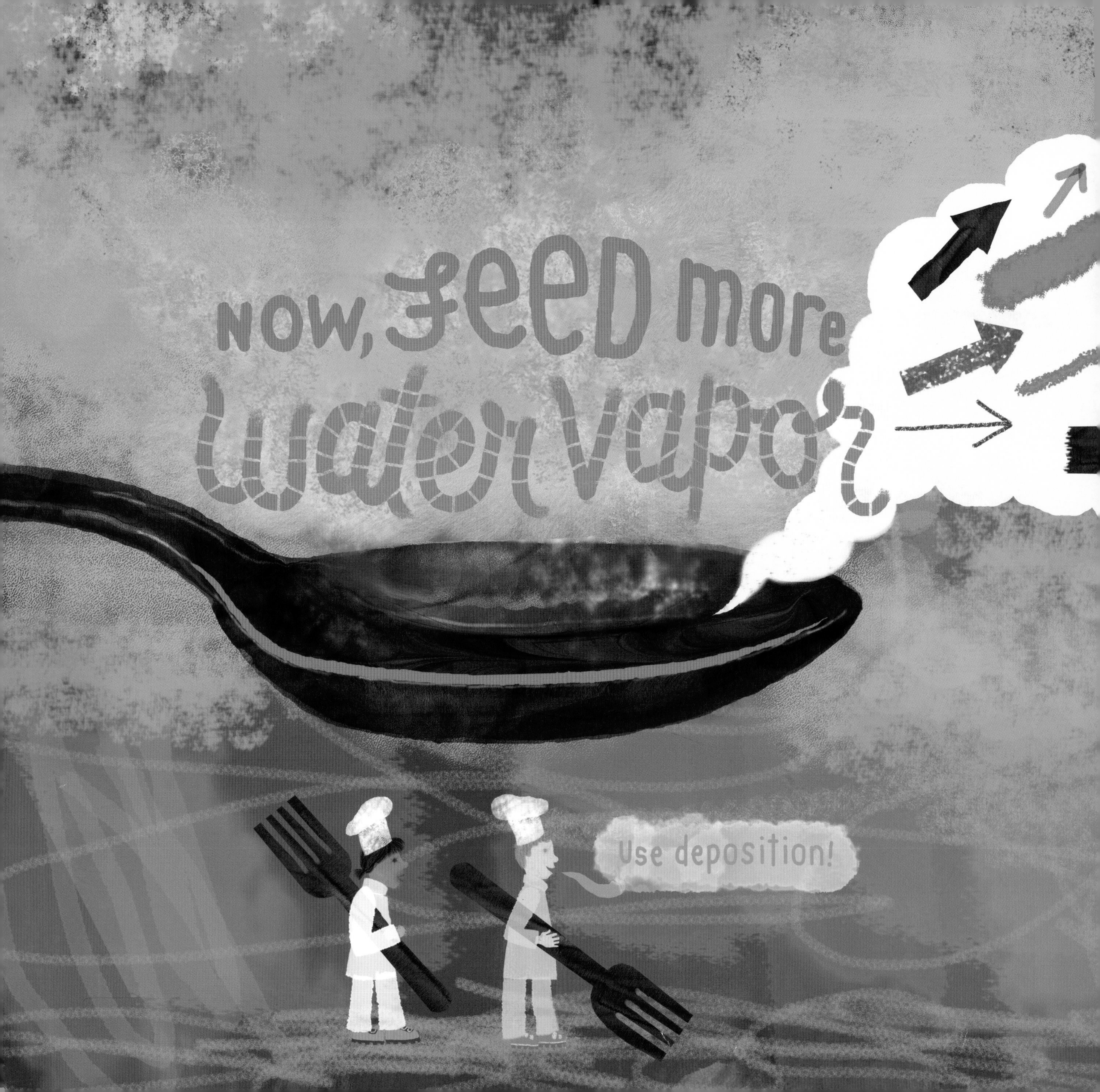

to each snow crystal.

or by adding
or subtracting
water
vapor,

you can make
different
snow crystal shapes,
like

STELLAR DENDRITES, which also grow at about -15°C (5°F).

NEEDLES, which grow at about -5°C (23°F).

STELLAR DENDRITES, which grow at about -2°C (28°F).

STELLAR PLATES, which also grow at about -15°C (5°F).

STELLAR PLATES, which grow at about -2°C (28°F).

THIN PLATES, which also grow from -10°C to -22°C (14°F to -8°F).

THIN PLATES, which grow at about -2°C (28°F).

COLUMNS, which grow from -5°C to -8°C (23°F to 18°F).

THICK PLATES, which also grow at -10°C (14°F) and colder.

0°C	-5°C	-10°C	-15°C	-20
32°F	23°F	14°F	5°F	-

COLUMNS,
which also grow at -22°C (-8°F) and colder.

MOST
WATER
VAPOR

MORE
WATER
VAPOR

SOME
WATER
VAPOR

| -25 C | -30 C | -35 C | -40 C |
| -13 F | -22 F | -31 F | -40 F |

Meanwhile, high in the clouds...

Forget the clouds! I'm the star of the show.

Why can't I be in this shot?

I work my fingers to the stick!

CRASHING! Condensing!

Evaporating! FREEZING!

I'm black-and-blue and airsick and....

Roll commercial!
Chef's having a meltdown!

We interrupt this broadcast for a commercial break.

BRRR YOUR ARCTIC TV

this episode of

The Snow

Show

brought to you

by

POLAR POPS!

CHILL your CHOPS!

NOW, back to our regular program....

Add one quintillion

more water vapor molecules to each snow crystal.

That's 1 with 18 zeros after it.

Or 1,000,
000,
000,
000,
000,
000.

I can't even count to one quintillion!

I dran
one quintillic
chocolate mi
molecule
at breakfas

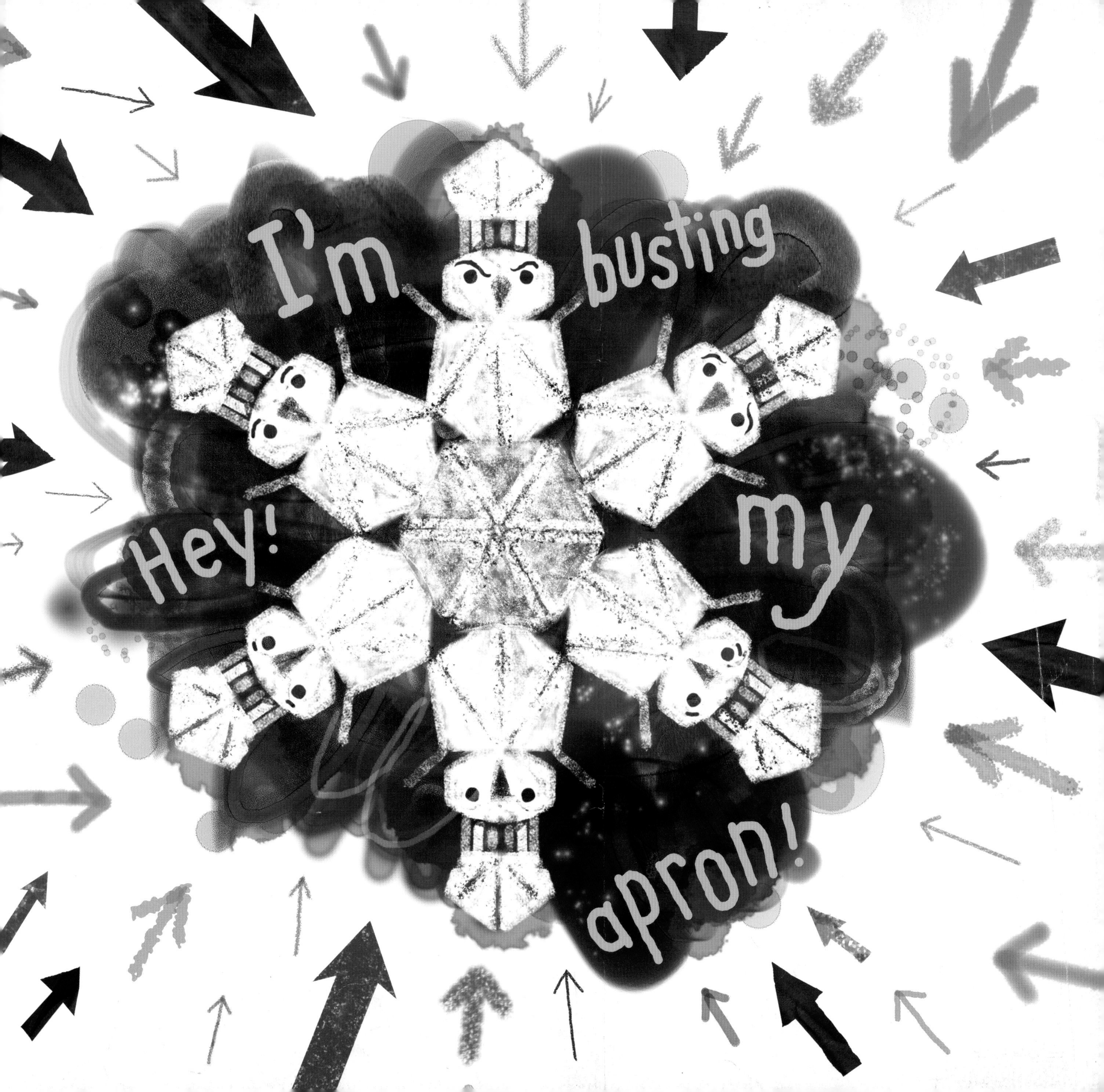

Hey! I'm busting my apron!

When the snow crystals get heavy,

w h o o o o

This is the control tower, Chef Kelvin. You are cleared to land.

let them fall from the clouds to the ground.

Roll into balls.

Stack, if desired.

And this time,
make my muscles BIG!

Repeat as necessary.

Serve immediately.

APPLAUSE!

Food fight!

rom everyone here at The Snow Show,
hanks for tuning in.
May all of your days
be snow days!

That's a wrap!

SNOW/Fisher
SCENE 121 TAKE 42
D. CAM
DATE: DECEMBER

PRODUCER: Carolyn Fisher   BEST BOY: Steve Arthur

INTERN: Geneva   GRIP: Kathryn Molcak

STUNTS: Michael Fisher   GAFFER: Jim Fisher

CAMERA: Beth Fisher   WRANGLER: Christina Reynolds

PROMPTER: Allyn Johnston   SCRIPT SUPERVISOR: Andrea Welch

Requests for permission to make copies of any part of the work
should be submitted online at www.harcourt.com/contact or mailed
to the following address: Permissions Department, Harcourt, Inc.,
6277 Sea Harbor Drive, Orlando, Florida 32887-6777.

www.HarcourtBooks.com

Library of Congress Cataloging-in-Publication Data
Fisher, Carolyn, 1968—
The snow show/[written and illustrated by] Carolyn Fisher.
p.   cm.
Summary: A cooking show goes on location to the North Pole to
demonstrate the recipe for making snow.
[1. Snow—Fiction.   2. Cookery—Fiction.   3. Television
broadcasting—Fiction.]   I. Title.
PZ7.F4994Sn   2008
[Fic]—dc22   2007031724
ISBN 978-0-15-206019-0

First edition
H G F E D C B A

The illustrations in this book were created digitally.
The display and text lettering were created by Carolyn Fisher.
Color separations by Colourscan Co. Pte. Ltd., Singapore
Manufactured by South China Printing Company, Ltd., China
Production supervision by Christine Witnik
Designed by Carolyn Fisher and Michele Wetherbee

Deleted Scenes

Snow Stars

Wilson "Snowflake" Bentley, a farmer who lived in Vermont, took the first photograph of a snowflake through a microscope in 1885, when he was nineteen years old. Over Bentley's lifetime, he took thousands of photos of snow crystals.

Ukichiro Nakaya, a Japanese scientist, began studying snow in the 1930s. He invented a system to classify the different snow crystal shapes. Nakaya was also the first scientist to grow artificial snowflakes inside a lab.

SNOW CRYSTAL or SNOW FLAKE?

A snow crystal is a single ice crystal. A snowflake could be a single crystal, or a cluster of snow crystals hitched loosely together.

Further Reading

Libbrecht, Ken. KEN LIBBRECHT's FIELD GUIDE to SNOWFLAKES. Stillwater, Minn.: Voyageur Press, 2006.

Libbrecht, Ken. THE SNOWFLAKE: WINTER's SECRET BEAUTY. Stillwater, Minn.: Voyageur Press, 2003.

SnowCrystals.com
www.its.caltech.edu/~atomic/snowcrystals/

Make your own POLAR POPS!
(serves 6)

Ingredients

2 cups polar bear milk (If you can't find polar bear milk, use vanilla yogurt instea[d])
1 cup raspberries
6 5-oz. waxy paper cups
6 Popsicle sticks

Directions

1. Stir the raspberries into the polar bear milk (or yogurt).

2. Fill the paper cups about halfway with the mixture.

3. Set the cups on a plate or t[ray]

4. Cover each cup with alumin[um] foil, then poke a Popsicle st[ick] through the center of the fo[il] and into the mixture.

5. Freeze until solid (about four hours).

6. To serve, remove the foil and peel away the cups.

Enjoy!

Phase CHANGES

EVAPORATION:	liquid + heat = vapor (gas)
CONDENSATION:	vapor − heat = liquid
FREEZING:	liquid − heat = solid (ice)
MELTING:	solid + heat = liquid
DEPOSITION:	vapor − heat = solid
SUBLIMATION:	solid + heat = vapor

BONUS SNOW CRYSTALS

POLYCRYSTALS:
(composed of several crystals growing in all directions)

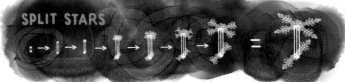

RADIATING PLATES   **RADIATING DENDRITES**

BULLETS

IRREGULARS

DIAMOND DUST
(the tiniest crystals, also called prisms)

CAPPED COLUMNS

SPLIT STARS

SECTORED PLATES
(stellar plates that are divided into wedges, like pieces of pie)

TRIANGULAR CRYSTALS

DOUBLE STARS

SPLIT PLATES

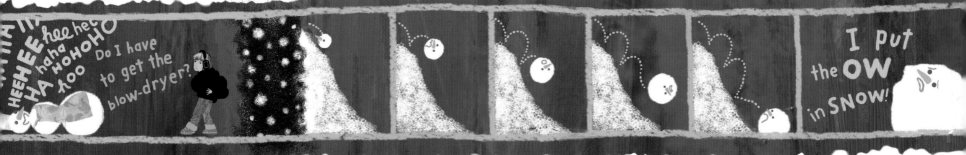

BLOOPERS

Will somebody put me TOGETHER?

Very funny.

Wiseguys.

HAHAHA HEE HEE hee hee HA HO HO HO hoo Do I have to get the blow-dryer?

I put the **OW** in SNOW!

CUT! I can't see the teleprompter without my...

...glasses!